BRIGHT IDEA BOOKS

AMAZING HUMAN FEATS OF
Strength

by Debbie Vilardi

raintree

a Capstone company — publishers for children

Raintree is an imprint of Capstone Global Library Limited, a company incorporated in England and Wales having its registered office at 264 Banbury Road, Oxford, OX2 7DY – Registered company number: 6695582

www.raintree.co.uk
myorders@raintree.co.uk

Edited by Meg Gaertner
Designed by Becky Daum
Production by Craig Hinton
Originated by Capstone Global Library Ltd
Printed and bound in India

ISBN 978 1 4747 7520 5   ISBN 978 1 4747 7344 7
22 21 20 19 18   23 22 21 20 19
10 9 8 7 6 5 4 3 2 1   10 9 8 7 6 5 4 3 2 1

British Library Cataloguing in Publication Data
A full catalogue record for this book is available from the British Library.

Acknowledgements
We would like to thank the following for permission to reproduce photographs: Alamy: Michael Wright/WENN Ltd, 17; Getty Images: Matt Roberts/Getty Images Sport, 27, Ruaridh Connellan/Barcroft USA/Barcroft Media, 23; iStockphoto: aluxum, 5, lagunaguiance, cover (foreground); Newscom: Kevin Dietsch/UPI, 7, Kieran Galvin/NurPhoto/Sipa USA, 13, Rachen Sageamsak/Xinhua News Agency, 10–11, Zhang Yongfeng/Xinhua News Agency, 18–19; Shutterstock Images: Asia Images Group, 24–25, balipadma, 9, 30–31, Oleksandr Zamurulev, 20–21, Parinya, cover (background), Stefan Holm, 14–15. Design Elements: iStockphoto, Red Line Editorial, and Shutterstock Images.

CONTENTS

STRENGTH

A woman lifts more than twice her weight. A man pulls a plane behind him. A woman wins 13 world titles in arm wrestling.

People show their strength in many ways. Their strength helps them to do amazing things.

Some rock climbers achieve amazing feats in their sport.

HEAVY
Lifting

Kuo Hsing-Chun weighs only 58 kilograms (9 stone). But she can lift more than twice her weight. She competed in Taiwan in 2017.

HEAVYWEIGHT

Olympic weight-lifting has two forms. The first is the **snatch**. The second is the **clean and jerk**.

First, she snatched 107 kilograms (236 pounds). She won the event. Then she lifted 142 kilograms (313 pounds) to her chest. Then she raised it over her head. She won the clean and jerk. She also broke the world record.

Hsing-Chun won bronze at the 2016 Olympics.

CHAPTER 3

POWERFUL
Pastor

Kevin Fast is a Canadian **pastor**. He is very strong. Fast began lifting weights when he was 12 years old. Now he trains in new ways. He lifts tractor tyres. He pulls his truck up a hill.

Fast has set many world records.
One was for the heaviest truck pulled
over 30.5 metres (100 feet). Another was
for the heaviest house pulled. Many of his
records are still unbroken.

Athletes pull vehicles in **strongman** competitions.

Fast pulled
another plane
in 2014 in Thailand.

PULLING A PLANE

One of Fast's biggest feats was in 2009. He set out to pull a plane. The plane weighed 188,830 kilograms (416,299 pounds).

At first the plane did not move. Fast was getting tired. But he did not give up. The plane moved after about 45 seconds. He pulled the plane more than 8.8 metres (28 feet).

CHAPTER 4

CARIBBEAN
Champion

Akeem Stewart is from Trinidad and Tobago in the Caribbean. One of his legs is longer than the other. He competes in the **Paralympics**.

He competes in the **javelin** and **shot put**. Athletes throw objects in both these events. They throw as far as they can.

SHOT PUT

The shot is a metal ball. It weighs 7.26 kilograms (16.01 pounds) for men. Women throw a 4-kilogram (8.8-pound) ball.

Stewart gets ready to throw.

An athlete runs a set distance before throwing the javelin.

RECORD THROWS

Stewart won gold at the 2016 Paralympics. He broke the world record in javelin. His longest throw was 57.32 metres (188.06 feet).

Stewart also holds the world record for shot put. His longest throw was 19.08 metres (62.6 feet).

PARALYMPICS

Paralympic athletes compete against others with similar disabilities. This keeps events fair.

CHAPTER 5

STRONGMAN

Eddie Hall was the World's Strongest Man (WSM) in 2017. It took him 10 years to win this title. He first worked as a truck driver. But he wanted to be a full-time strongman.

Hall found a **sponsor**. He worked out a lot. He ate 12,000 calories per day. He weighed more than 181 kilograms (28 stone) in 2018.

Hall is nicknamed "The Beast".

Men lift cars at some strongman competitions.

THE COMPETITION

The WSM is a competition. It happens every year. Men compete in many events. They lift huge rocks onto high platforms. They pull planes and buses.

Athletes also do the **dead lift**. Hall set the world record in 2016. He lifted 500 kilograms (1,102 pounds).

THE COST

Being the strongest has its costs.

The dead lift nearly killed Hall in 2016.

He bled from his eyes, ears and nose.

For a few days he lost his sight. His back

was bruised for two weeks.

Hall recovered. He trained for the 2017 WSM and won the title.

In the dead lift, athletes pick up a heavy bar from the ground.

CHAPTER 6

A WINNING
Family

Some families cycle together. Others like to go camping. Joyce, Jessica and Josie King like to arm wrestle. They also like to win.

The Kings are champion arm
wrestlers. Jessica King has won
two world titles. But she's never beaten
her mother, Joyce.

Josie (left), Joyce
(middle) and Jessica
(right) lift weights
to train.

Champion arm wrestlers need strength and good technique.

AS A FAMILY

Joyce King is a 13-time world champion. Josie is Joyce's granddaughter. She has competed in Canada. She has two gold medals.

Arm wrestling takes great strength. The King women often train together. They eat food with lots of protein. They practise their arm wrestling form.

CHAPTER 7

SUMO Champion

Two sumo wrestlers stand in a ring. They cannot leave the circle. Only their feet can touch the ground. The men try to push each other out of the ring. They try to force each other to the ground.

Sumo wrestling is Japan's national sport. But for many years the champion was not Japanese. Japanese Kisenosato Yutaka won a tournament in January 2017. He won again in March. He earned the **yokozuna** rank. Japan celebrated its national champion.

Kisenosato Yutaka greets fans at a sumo wrestling event.

GLOSSARY

clean and jerk
weight-lifting event in which athletes bring the weight to their shoulders before lifting it overhead

dead lift
weight-lifting event in which athletes pick up metal bars weighted with heavy plates

javelin
light spear that is thrown for sport

Paralympics
major sporting competition in which athletes with disabilities compete

pastor
person in charge of a Christian church

retire
leave one's previous job to work at something else or to not work at all

shot put
sporting event in which athletes throw a heavy round object as far as they can

snatch
weight-lifting event in which athletes lift the weight overhead in a single motion

sponsor
person or organization that provides money for an event or activity

strongman
man who competes in events involving strength

yokozuna
highest rank possible in sumo wrestling

OTHER AMAZING FEATS

- Donna Moore was the World's Strongest Woman in 2016 and 2017. She also claimed a world record. She lifted a massive stone weighing 147 kilograms (324 pounds) over a 1.1-metre (44-inch) bar. She did this twice.

- Naomi Kutin could lift 98 kilograms (215 pounds) by the age of 9. At 16, she was lifting more than 159 kilograms (350 pounds).

- Alex Honnold climbed the El Capitan rock face in Yosemite National Park, USA. He climbed the 914 metres (3,000 feet) without a harness or rope. The climb took approximately four hours.

ACTIVITY

WRITE A PROFILE

Choose one of the people featured in this book. Research his or her feat. You can use online sources to learn about the athlete. You can borrow books from your local library. Write a profile or make a video about the athlete. Some questions you might consider are:

- Why does this person compete in the event? What motivates this person?

- What makes the event this person competes in particularly challenging?

- How does this person train to be so strong?

- What makes this person inspiring?

31

FIND OUT MORE

Curious about the science behind strength? Check out these resources:

Books

Extreme Athletes (Ultimate Adventurers) Charlotte Guillain (Raintree, 2014)

My Amazing Body Machine, Robert Winston (DK Children, 2017)

Record Breakers!, DK (DK Children, 2018)

The Skeleton and Muscles (Flowchart Science: The Human Body), Louise and Richard Spilsbury (Raintree, 2018)

Websites

Find out more about athletics.
www.dkfindout.com/uk/sports/athletics

Find out more about your amazing body.
www.dkfindout.com/uk/human-body/your-amazing-body

INDEX